THE UNIVERSITY OF
WINCHESTER

Martial Rose Library
Tel: 01962 827306

To be returned on or before the day marked above, subject to recall.

Cadenus And Vanessa

Table of Contents

Cadenus And Vanessa

Jonathan Swift

WRITTEN ANNO 1713.

THE shepherds and the nymphs were seen
Pleading before the Cyprian Queen.
The counsel for the fair began
Accusing the false creature, man.
The brief with weighty crimes was charged,
On which the pleader much enlarged:
That Cupid now has lost his art,
Or blunts the point of every dart;
His altar now no longer smokes;
His mother's aid no youth invokes—
This tempts free–thinkers to refine,
And bring in doubt their powers divine,
Now love is dwindled to intrigue,
And marriage grown a money–league.
Which crimes aforesaid (with her leave)
Were (as he humbly did conceive)
Against our Sovereign Lady's peace,
Against the statutes in that case,
Against her dignity and crown:
Then prayed an answer and sat down.

Cadenus And Vanessa

The nymphs with scorn beheld their foes:
When the defendant's counsel rose,
And, what no lawyer ever lacked,
With impudence owned all the fact.
But, what the gentlest heart would vex,
Laid all the fault on t'other sex.
That modern love is no such thing
As what those ancient poets sing;
A fire celestial, chaste, refined,
Conceived and kindled in the mind,
Which having found an equal flame,
Unites, and both become the same,
In different breasts together burn,
Together both to ashes turn.
But women now feel no such fire,
And only know the gross desire;
Their passions move in lower spheres,
Where'er caprice or folly steers.
A dog, a parrot, or an ape,
Or some worse brute in human shape
Engross the fancies of the fair,
The few soft moments they can spare
From visits to receive and pay,
From scandal, politics, and play,
From fans, and flounces, and brocades,
From equipage and park—parades,
From all the thousand female toys,
From every trifle that employs
The out or inside of their heads
Between their toilets and their beds.
In a dull stream, which, moving slow,
You hardly see the current flow,
If a small breeze obstructs the course,
It whirls about for want of force,
And in its narrow circle gathers
Nothing but chaff, and straws, and feathers:

Cadenus And Vanessa

The current of a female mind
Stops thus, and turns with every wind;
Thus whirling round, together draws
Fools, fops, and rakes, for chaff and straws.
Hence we conclude, no women's hearts
Are won by virtue, wit, and parts;
Nor are the men of sense to blame
For breasts incapable of flame:
The fault must on the nymphs be placed,
Grown so corrupted in their taste.
The pleader having spoke his best,
Had witness ready to attest,
Who fairly could on oath depose,
When questions on the fact arose,
That every article was true;
NOR FURTHER THOSE DEPONENTS KNEW:
Therefore he humbly would insist,
The bill might be with costs dismissed.
The cause appeared of so much weight,
That Venus from the judgment-seat
Desired them not to talk so loud,
Else she must interpose a cloud:
For if the heavenly folk should know
These pleadings in the Courts below,
That mortals here disdain to love,
She ne'er could show her face above.
For gods, their betters, are too wise
To value that which men despise.
"And then," said she, "my son and I
Must stroll in air 'twixt earth and sky:
Or else, shut out from heaven and earth,
Fly to the sea, my place of birth;
There live with daggled mermaids pent,
And keep on fish perpetual Lent."
But since the case appeared so nice,
She thought it best to take advice.

3

Cadenus And Vanessa

The Muses, by their king's permission,
Though foes to love, attend the session,
And on the right hand took their places
In order; on the left, the Graces:
To whom she might her doubts propose
On all emergencies that rose.
The Muses oft were seen to frown;
The Graces half ashamed look down;
And 'twas observed, there were but few
Of either sex, among the crew,
Whom she or her assessors knew.
The goddess soon began to see
Things were not ripe for a decree,
And said she must consult her books,
The lovers' Fletas, Bractons, Cokes.
First to a dapper clerk she beckoned,
To turn to Ovid, book the second;
She then referred them to a place
In Virgil (VIDE Dido's case);
As for Tibullus's reports,
They never passed for law in Courts:
For Cowley's brief, and pleas of Waller,
Still their authority is smaller.
There was on both sides much to say;
She'd hear the cause another day;
And so she did, and then a third,
She heard it— there she kept her word;
But with rejoinders and replies,
Long bills, and answers, stuffed with lies
Demur, imparlance, and essoign,
The parties ne'er could issue join:
For sixteen years the cause was spun,
And then stood where it first begun.
Now, gentle Clio, sing or say,
What Venus meant by this delay.
The goddess, much perplexed in mind,

Cadenus And Vanessa

To see her empire thus declined,
When first this grand debate arose
Above her wisdom to compose,
Conceived a project in her head,
To work her ends; which, if it sped,
Would show the merits of the cause
Far better than consulting laws.
In a glad hour Lucina's aid
Produced on earth a wondrous maid,
On whom the queen of love was bent
To try a new experiment.
She threw her law–books on the shelf,
And thus debated with herself:–
"Since men allege they ne'er can find
Those beauties in a female mind
Which raise a flame that will endure
For ever, uncorrupt and pure;
If 'tis with reason they complain,
This infant shall restore my reign.
I'll search where every virtue dwells,
From Courts inclusive down to cells.
What preachers talk, or sages write,
These I will gather and unite,
And represent them to mankind
Collected in that infant's mind."
This said, she plucks in heaven's high bowers
A sprig of Amaranthine flowers,
In nectar thrice infuses bays,
Three times refined in Titan's rays:
Then calls the Graces to her aid,
And sprinkles thrice the now–born maid.
From whence the tender skin assumes
A sweetness above all perfumes;
From whence a cleanliness remains,
Incapable of outward stains;
From whence that decency of mind,

Cadenus And Vanessa

So lovely in a female kind.
Where not one careless thought intrudes
Less modest than the speech of prudes;
Where never blush was called in aid,
The spurious virtue in a maid,
A virtue but at second–hand;
They blush because they understand.
The Graces next would act their part,
And show but little of their art;
Their work was half already done,
The child with native beauty shone,
The outward form no help required:
Each breathing on her thrice, inspired
That gentle, soft, engaging air
Which in old times adorned the fair,
And said, "Vanessa be the name
By which thou shalt be known to fame;
Vanessa, by the gods enrolled:
Her name on earth— shall not be told."
But still the work was not complete,
When Venus thought on a deceit:
Drawn by her doves, away she flies,
And finds out Pallas in the skies:
Dear Pallas, I have been this morn
To see a lovely infant born:
A boy in yonder isle below,
So like my own without his bow,
By beauty could your heart be won,
You'd swear it is Apollo's son;
But it shall ne'er be said, a child
So hopeful has by me been spoiled;
I have enough besides to spare,
And give him wholly to your care.
Wisdom's above suspecting wiles;
The queen of learning gravely smiles,
Down from Olympus comes with joy,

Cadenus And Vanessa

Mistakes Vanessa for a boy;
Then sows within her tender mind
Seeds long unknown to womankind;
For manly bosoms chiefly fit,
The seeds of knowledge, judgment, wit,
Her soul was suddenly endued
With justice, truth, and fortitude;
With honour, which no breath can stain,
Which malice must attack in vain:
With open heart and bounteous hand:
But Pallas here was at a stand;
She know in our degenerate days
Bare virtue could not live on praise,
That meat must be with money bought:
She therefore, upon second thought,
Infused yet as it were by stealth,
Some small regard for state and wealth:
Of which as she grew up there stayed
A tincture in the prudent maid:
She managed her estate with care,
Yet liked three footmen to her chair,
But lest he should neglect his studies
Like a young heir, the thrifty goddess
(For fear young master should be spoiled)
Would use him like a younger child;
And, after long computing, found
'Twould come to just five thousand pound.
The Queen of Love was pleased and proud
To we Vanessa thus endowed;
She doubted not but such a dame
Through every breast would dart a flame;
That every rich and lordly swain
With pride would drag about her chain;
That scholars would forsake their books
To study bright Vanessa's looks:
As she advanced that womankind

7

Cadenus And Vanessa

Would by her model form their mind,
And all their conduct would be tried
By her, as an unerring guide.
Offending daughters oft would hear
Vanessa's praise rung in their ear:
Miss Betty, when she does a fault,
Lets fall her knife, or spills the salt,
Will thus be by her mother chid,
"'Tis what Vanessa never did."
Thus by the nymphs and swains adored,
My power shall be again restored,
And happy lovers bless my reign—
So Venus hoped, but hoped in vain.
For when in time the martial maid
Found out the trick that Venus played,
She shakes her helm, she knits her brows,
And fired with indignation, vows
To—morrow, ere the setting sun,
She'd all undo that she had done.
But in the poets we may find
A wholesome law, time out of mind,
Had been confirmed by Fate's decree;
That gods, of whatso'er degree,
Resume not what themselves have given,
Or any brother—god in Heaven;
Which keeps the peace among the gods,
Or they must always be at odds.
And Pallas, if she broke the laws,
Must yield her foe the stronger cause;
A shame to one so much adored
For Wisdom, at Jove's council—board.
Besides, she feared the queen of love
Would meet with better friends above.
And though she must with grief reflect
To see a mortal virgin deck'd
With graces hitherto unknown

Cadenus And Vanessa

To female breasts, except her own,
Yet she would act as best became
A goddess of unspotted fame;
She knew, by augury divine,
Venus would fail in her design:
She studied well the point, and found
Her foe's conclusions were not sound,
From premises erroneous brought,
And therefore the deduction's nought,
And must have contrary effects
To what her treacherous foe expects.
In proper season Pallas meets
The queen of love, whom thus she greets
(For Gods, we are by Homer told,
Can in celestial language scold),
"Perfidious Goddess! but in vain
You formed this project in your brain,
A project for thy talents fit,
With much deceit, and little wit;
Thou hast, as thou shalt quickly see,
Deceived thyself instead of me;
For how can heavenly wisdom prove
An instrument to earthly love?
Know'st thou not yet that men commence
Thy votaries, for want of sense?
Nor shall Vanessa be the theme
To manage thy abortive scheme;
She'll prove the greatest of thy foes,
And yet I scorn to interpose,
But using neither skill nor force,
Leave all things to their natural course."
The goddess thus pronounced her doom,
When, lo, Vanessa in her bloom,
Advanced like Atalanta's star,
But rarely seen, and seen from far:
In a new world with caution stepped,

Watched all the company she kept,
Well knowing from the books she read
What dangerous paths young virgins tread;
Would seldom at the park appear,
Nor saw the play–house twice a year;
Yet not incurious, was inclined
To know the converse of mankind.
First issued from perfumers' shops
A crowd of fashionable fops;
They liked her how she liked the play?
Then told the tattle of the day,
A duel fought last night at two
About a lady— you know who;
Mentioned a new Italian, come
Either from Muscovy or Rome;
Gave hints of who and who's together;
Then fell to talking of the weather:
Last night was so extremely fine,
The ladies walked till after nine.
Then in soft voice, and speech absurd,
With nonsense every second word,
With fustian from exploded plays,
They celebrate her beauty's praise,
Run o'er their cant of stupid lies,
And tell the murders of her eyes.
With silent scorn Vanessa sat,
Scarce list'ning to their idle chat;
Further than sometimes by a frown,
When they grew pert, to pull them down.
At last she spitefully was bent
To try their wisdom's full extent;
And said, she valued nothing less
Than titles, figure, shape, and dress;
That merit should be chiefly placed
In judgment, knowledge, wit, and taste;
And these, she offered to dispute,

Cadenus And Vanessa

Alone distinguished man from brute:
That present times have no pretence
To virtue, in the noble sense
By Greeks and Romans understood,
To perish for our country's good.
She named the ancient heroes round,
Explained for what they were renowned;
Then spoke with censure, or applause,
Of foreign customs, rites, and laws;
Through nature and through art she ranged,
And gracefully her subject changed:
In vain; her hearers had no share
In all she spoke, except to stare.
Their judgment was upon the whole,
— That lady is the dullest soul—
Then tipped their forehead in a jeer,
As who should say— she wants it here;
She may be handsome, young, and rich,
But none will burn her for a witch.
A party next of glittering dames,
From round the purlieus of St. James,
Came early, out of pure goodwill,
To see the girl in deshabille.
Their clamour 'lighting from their chairs,
Grew louder, all the way up stairs;
At entrance loudest, where they found
The room with volumes littered round,
Vanessa held Montaigne, and read,
Whilst Mrs. Susan combed her head:
They called for tea and chocolate,
And fell into their usual chat,
Discoursing with important face,
On ribbons, fans, and gloves, and lace:
Showed patterns just from India brought,
And gravely asked her what she thought,
Whether the red or green were best,

Cadenus And Vanessa

And what they cost? Vanessa guessed,
As came into her fancy first,
Named half the rates, and liked the worst.
To scandal next— What awkward thing
Was that, last Sunday, in the ring?
I'm sorry Mopsa breaks so fast;
I said her face would never last,
Corinna with that youthful air,
Is thirty, and a bit to spare.
Her fondness for a certain earl
Began, when I was but a girl.
Phyllis, who but a month ago
Was married to the Tunbridge beau,
I saw coquetting t'other night
In public with that odious knight.
They rallied next Vanessa's dress;
That gown was made for old Queen Bess.
Dear madam, let me set your head;
Don't you intend to put on red?
A petticoat without a hoop!
Sure, you are not ashamed to stoop;
With handsome garters at your knees,
No matter what a fellow sees.
Filled with disdain, with rage inflamed,
Both of herself and sex ashamed,
The nymph stood silent out of spite,
Nor would vouchsafe to set them right.
Away the fair detractors went,
And gave, by turns, their censures vent.
She's not so handsome in my eyes:
For wit, I wonder where it lies.
She's fair and clean, and that's the most;
But why proclaim her for a toast?
A baby face, no life, no airs,
But what she learnt at country fairs.
Scarce knows what difference is between

Cadenus And Vanessa

Rich Flanders lace, and Colberteen.
I'll undertake my little Nancy,
In flounces has a better fancy.
With all her wit, I would not ask
Her judgment, how to buy a mask.
We begged her but to patch her face,
She never hit one proper place;
Which every girl at five years old
Can do as soon as she is told.
I own, that out–of–fashion stuff
Becomes the creature well enough.
The girl might pass, if we could get her
To know the world a little better.
(TO KNOW THE WORLD! a modern phrase
For visits, ombre, balls, and plays.)
Thus, to the world's perpetual shame,
The queen of beauty lost her aim,
Too late with grief she understood
Pallas had done more harm than good;
For great examples are but vain,
Where ignorance begets disdain.
Both sexes, armed with guilt and spite,
Against Vanessa's power unite;
To copy her few nymphs aspired;
Her virtues fewer swains admired;
So stars, beyond a certain height,
Give mortals neither heat nor light.
Yet some of either sex, endowed
With gifts superior to the crowd,
With virtue, knowledge, taste, and wit,
She condescended to admit;
With pleasing arts she could reduce
Men's talents to their proper use;
And with address each genius hold
To that wherein it most excelled;
Thus making others' wisdom known,

13

Cadenus And Vanessa

Could please them and improve her own.
A modest youth said something new,
She placed it in the strongest view.
All humble worth she strove to raise;
Would not be praised, yet loved to praise.
The learned met with free approach,
Although they came not in a coach.
Some clergy too she would allow,
Nor quarreled at their awkward bow.
But this was for Cadenus' sake;
A gownman of a different make.
Whom Pallas, once Vanessa's tutor,
Had fixed on for her coadjutor.
But Cupid, full of mischief, longs
To vindicate his mother's wrongs.
On Pallas all attempts are vain;
One way he knows to give her pain;
Vows on Vanessa's heart to take
Due vengeance, for her patron's sake.
Those early seeds by Venus sown,
In spite of Pallas, now were grown;
And Cupid hoped they would improve
By time, and ripen into love.
The boy made use of all his craft,
In vain discharging many a shaft,
Pointed at colonels, lords, and beaux;
Cadenus warded off the blows,
For placing still some book betwixt,
The darts were in the cover fixed,
Or often blunted and recoiled,
On Plutarch's morals struck, were spoiled.
The queen of wisdom could foresee,
But not prevent the Fates decree;
And human caution tries in vain
To break that adamantine chain.
Vanessa, though by Pallas taught,

Cadenus And Vanessa

By love invulnerable thought,
Searching in books for wisdom's aid,
Was, in the very search, betrayed.
Cupid, though all his darts were lost,
Yet still resolved to spare no cost;
He could not answer to his fame
The triumphs of that stubborn dame,
A nymph so hard to be subdued,
Who neither was coquette nor prude.
I find, says he, she wants a doctor,
Both to adore her, and instruct her:
I'll give her what she most admires,
Among those venerable sires.
Cadenus is a subject fit,
Grown old in politics and wit;
Caressed by Ministers of State,
Of half mankind the dread and hate.
Whate'er vexations love attend,
She need no rivals apprehend
Her sex, with universal voice,
Must laugh at her capricious choice.
Cadenus many things had writ,
Vanessa much esteemed his wit,
And called for his poetic works!
Meantime the boy in secret lurks.
And while the book was in her hand,
The urchin from his private stand
Took aim, and shot with all his strength
A dart of such prodigious length,
It pierced the feeble volume through,
And deep transfixed her bosom too.
Some lines, more moving than the rest,
Struck to the point that pierced her breast;
And, borne directly to the heart,
With pains unknown, increased her smart.
Vanessa, not in years a score,

Cadenus And Vanessa

Dreams of a gown of forty—four;
Imaginary charms can find,
In eyes with reading almost blind;
Cadenus now no more appears
Declined in health, advanced in years.
She fancies music in his tongue,
Nor farther looks, but thinks him young.
What mariner is not afraid
To venture in a ship decayed?
What planter will attempt to yoke
A sapling with a falling oak?
As years increase, she brighter shines,
Cadenus with each day declines,
And he must fall a prey to Time,
While she continues in her prime.
Cadenus, common forms apart,
In every scene had kept his heart;
Had sighed and languished, vowed and writ,
For pastime, or to show his wit;
But time, and books, and State affairs,
Had spoiled his fashionable airs,
He now could praise, esteem, approve,
But understood not what was love.
His conduct might have made him styled
A father, and the nymph his child.
That innocent delight he took
To see the virgin mind her book,
Was but the master's secret joy
In school to hear the finest boy.
Her knowledge with her fancy grew,
She hourly pressed for something new;
Ideas came into her mind
So fact, his lessons lagged behind;
She reasoned, without plodding long,
Nor ever gave her judgment wrong.
But now a sudden change was wrought,

Cadenus And Vanessa

She minds no longer what he taught.
Cadenus was amazed to find
Such marks of a distracted mind;
For though she seemed to listen more
To all he spoke, than e'er before.
He found her thoughts would absent range,
Yet guessed not whence could spring the change.
And first he modestly conjectures,
His pupil might be tired with lectures,
Which helped to mortify his pride,
Yet gave him not the heart to chide;
But in a mild dejected strain,
At last he ventured to complain:
Said, she should be no longer teased,
Might have her freedom when she pleased;
Was now convinced he acted wrong,
To hide her from the world so long,
And in dull studies to engage
One of her tender sex and age.
That every nymph with envy owned,
How she might shine in the GRANDE–MONDE,
And every shepherd was undone,
To see her cloistered like a nun.
This was a visionary scheme,
He waked, and found it but a dream;
A project far above his skill,
For Nature must be Nature still.
If she was bolder than became
A scholar to a courtly dame,
She might excuse a man of letters;
Thus tutors often treat their betters,
And since his talk offensive grew,
He came to take his last adieu.
Vanessa, filled with just disdain,
Would still her dignity maintain,
Instructed from her early years

Cadenus And Vanessa

To scorn the art of female tears.
Had he employed his time so long,
To teach her what was right or wrong,
Yet could such notions entertain,
That all his lectures were in vain?
She owned the wand'ring of her thoughts,
But he must answer for her faults.
She well remembered, to her cost,
That all his lessons were not lost.
Two maxims she could still produce,
And sad experience taught her use;
That virtue, pleased by being shown,
Knows nothing which it dare not own;
Can make us without fear disclose
Our inmost secrets to our foes;
That common forms were not designed
Directors to a noble mind.
Now, said the nymph, I'll let you see
My actions with your rules agree,
That I can vulgar forms despise,
And have no secrets to disguise.
I knew by what you said and writ,
How dangerous things were men of wit;
You cautioned me against their charms,
But never gave me equal arms;
Your lessons found the weakest part,
Aimed at the head, but reached the heart.
Cadenus felt within him rise
Shame, disappointment, guilt, surprise.
He know not how to reconcile
Such language, with her usual style:
And yet her words were so expressed,
He could not hope she spoke in jest.
His thoughts had wholly been confined
To form and cultivate her mind.
He hardly knew, till he was told,

Cadenus And Vanessa

Whether the nymph were young or old;
Had met her in a public place,
Without distinguishing her face,
Much less could his declining age
Vanessa's earliest thoughts engage.
And if her youth indifference met,
His person must contempt beget,
Or grant her passion be sincere,
How shall his innocence be clear?
Appearances were all so strong,
The world must think him in the wrong;
Would say he made a treach'rous use.
Of wit, to flatter and seduce;
The town would swear he had betrayed,
By magic spells, the harmless maid;
And every beau would have his jokes,
That scholars were like other folks;
That when Platonic flights were over,
The tutor turned a mortal lover.
So tender of the young and fair;
It showed a true paternal care—
Five thousand guineas in her purse;
The doctor might have fancied worst,—
Hardly at length he silence broke,
And faltered every word he spoke;
Interpreting her complaisance,
Just as a man sans consequence.
She rallied well, he always knew;
Her manner now was something new;
And what she spoke was in an air,
As serious as a tragic player.
But those who aim at ridicule,
Should fix upon some certain rule,
Which fairly hints they are in jest,
Else he must enter his protest;
For let a man be ne'er so wise,

Cadenus And Vanessa

He may be caught with sober lies;
A science which he never taught,
And, to be free, was dearly bought;
For, take it in its proper light,
'Tis just what coxcombs call a bite.
But not to dwell on things minute,
Vanessa finished the dispute,
Brought weighty arguments to prove,
That reason was her guide in love.
She thought he had himself described,
His doctrines when she fist imbibed;
What he had planted now was grown,
His virtues she might call her own;
As he approves, as he dislikes,
Love or contempt her fancy strikes.
Self—love in nature rooted fast,
Attends us first, and leaves us last:
Why she likes him, admire not at her,
She loves herself, and that's the matter.
How was her tutor wont to praise
The geniuses of ancient days!
(Those authors he so oft had named
For learning, wit, and wisdom famed).
Was struck with love, esteem, and awe,
For persons whom he never saw.
Suppose Cadenus flourished then,
He must adore such God—like men.
If one short volume could comprise
All that was witty, learned, and wise,
How would it be esteemed, and read,
Although the writer long were dead?
If such an author were alive,
How all would for his friendship strive;
And come in crowds to see his face?
And this she takes to be her case.
Cadenus answers every end,

Cadenus And Vanessa

The book, the author, and the friend,
The utmost her desires will reach,
Is but to learn what he can teach;
His converse is a system fit
Alone to fill up all her wit;
While ev'ry passion of her mind
In him is centred and confined.
Love can with speech inspire a mute,
And taught Vanessa to dispute.
This topic, never touched before,
Displayed her eloquence the more:
Her knowledge, with such pains acquired,
By this new passion grew inspired.
Through this she made all objects pass,
Which gave a tincture o'er the mass;
As rivers, though they bend and twine,
Still to the sea their course incline;
Or, as philosophers, who find
Some fav'rite system to their mind,
In every point to make it fit,
Will force all nature to submit.
Cadenus, who could ne'er suspect
His lessons would have such effect,
Or be so artfully applied,
Insensibly came on her side;
It was an unforeseen event,
Things took a turn he never meant.
Whoe'er excels in what we prize,
Appears a hero to our eyes;
Each girl, when pleased with what is taught,
Will have the teacher in her thought.
When miss delights in her spinnet,
A fiddler may a fortune get;
A blockhead, with melodious voice
In boarding—schools can have his choice;
And oft the dancing—master's art

Cadenus And Vanessa

Climbs from the toe to touch the heart.
In learning let a nymph delight,
The pedant gets a mistress by't.
Cadenus, to his grief and shame,
Could scarce oppose Vanessa's flame;
But though her arguments were strong,
At least could hardly with them wrong.
Howe'er it came, he could not tell,
But, sure, she never talked so well.
His pride began to interpose,
Preferred before a crowd of beaux,
So bright a nymph to come unsought,
Such wonder by his merit wrought;
'Tis merit must with her prevail,
He never know her judgment fail.
She noted all she ever read,
And had a most discerning head.
'Tis an old maxim in the schools,
That vanity's the food of fools;
Yet now and then your men of wit
Will condescend to take a bit.
So when Cadenus could not hide,
He chose to justify his pride;
Construing the passion she had shown,
Much to her praise, more to his own.
Nature in him had merit placed,
In her, a most judicious taste.
Love, hitherto a transient guest,
Ne'er held possession in his breast;
So long attending at the gate,
Disdain'd to enter in so late.
Love, why do we one passion call?
When 'tis a compound of them all;
Where hot and cold, where sharp and sweet,
In all their equipages meet;
Where pleasures mixed with pains appear,

Cadenus And Vanessa

Sorrow with joy, and hope with fear.
Wherein his dignity and age
Forbid Cadenus to engage.
But friendship in its greatest height,
A constant, rational delight,
On virtue's basis fixed to last,
When love's allurements long are past;
Which gently warms, but cannot burn;
He gladly offers in return;
His want of passion will redeem,
With gratitude, respect, esteem;
With that devotion we bestow,
When goddesses appear below.
While thus Cadenus entertains
Vanessa in exalted strains,
The nymph in sober words intreats
A truce with all sublime conceits.
For why such raptures, flights, and fancies,
To her who durst not read romances;
In lofty style to make replies,
Which he had taught her to despise?
But when her tutor will affect
Devotion, duty, and respect,
He fairly abdicates his throne,
The government is now her own;
He has a forfeiture incurred,
She vows to take him at his word,
And hopes he will not take it strange
If both should now their stations change
The nymph will have her turn, to be
The tutor; and the pupil he:
Though she already can discern
Her scholar is not apt to learn;
Or wants capacity to reach
The science she designs to teach;
Wherein his genius was below

Cadenus And Vanessa

The skill of every common beau;
Who, though he cannot spell, is wise
Enough to read a lady's eyes?
And will each accidental glance
Interpret for a kind advance.
But what success Vanessa met
Is to the world a secret yet;
Whether the nymph, to please her swain,
Talks in a high romantic strain;
Or whether he at last descends
To like with less seraphic ends;
Or to compound the bus'ness, whether
They temper love and books together;
Must never to mankind be told,
Nor shall the conscious muse unfold.
Meantime the mournful queen of love
Led but a weary life above.
She ventures now to leave the skies,
Grown by Vanessa's conduct wise.
For though by one perverse event
Pallas had crossed her first intent,
Though her design was not obtained,
Yet had she much experience gained;
And, by the project vainly tried,
Could better now the cause decide.
She gave due notice that both parties,
CORAM REGINA PROX' DIE MARTIS,
Should at their peril without fail
Come and appear, and save their bail.
All met, and silence thrice proclaimed,
One lawyer to each side was named.
The judge discovered in her face
Resentments for her late disgrace;
And, full of anger, shame, and grief,
Directed them to mind their brief;
Nor spend their time to show their reading,

Cadenus And Vanessa

She'd have a summary proceeding.
She gathered under every head,
The sum of what each lawyer said;
Gave her own reasons last; and then
Decreed the cause against the men.
But, in a weighty case like this,
To show she did not judge amiss,
Which evil tongues might else report,
She made a speech in open court;
Wherein she grievously complains,
"How she was cheated by the swains."
On whose petition (humbly showing
That women were not worth the wooing,
And that unless the sex would mend,
The race of lovers soon must end);
"She was at Lord knows what expense,
To form a nymph of wit and sense;
A model for her sex designed,
Who never could one lover find,
She saw her favour was misplaced;
The follows had a wretched taste;
She needs must tell them to their face,
They were a senseless, stupid race;
And were she to begin again,
She'd study to reform the men;
Or add some grains of folly more
To women than they had before.
To put them on an equal foot;
And this, or nothing else, would do't.
This might their mutual fancy strike,
Since every being loves its like.
But now, repenting what was done,
She left all business to her son;
She puts the world in his possession,
And let him use it at discretion."
The crier was ordered to dismiss

Cadenus And Vanessa

The court, so made his last O yes!
The goddess would no longer wait,
But rising from her chair of state,
Left all below at six and seven,
Harnessed her doves, and flew to Heaven.

CPSIA information can be obtained
at www.ICGtesting.com
Printed in the USA
LVOW09s1811220217

525093LV00004B/241/P